quartet

Also by David Kelly
Book (Eaglemont Press, 2021)
planes, birds, cats, things (Ginninderra Press, 2021)
the handyman and other poems (Ginninderra Press, 2023)

David Kelly

quartet

Acknowledgements

Some of these poems have been published in
the *Australian Poetry Journal*, *tamba*, the *Shepparton News*
and *finding my feet* (MPU anthology 2024).

Quartet
ISBN 978 1 76109 684 6
Copyright © text David Kelly 2024
Cover image: *Jupiter* – dennisspiteri.com.au

First published 2024 by
GINNINDERRA PRESS
PO Box 3461 Port Adelaide 5015
www.ginninderrapress.com.au

For my father, mother and brother
with thanks for the happy.

Contents

1 paragraphs	9
Giant leap	11
It's deep	12
Supermarket monkeys	13
Old men and little dogs	14
Orange-bellied Parrot	15
Clawdette	16
Green gate	17
Heart of orange	18
Scabs	19
Euroa green	20
Do they know	21
Scooter trains	22
Poetry requisites	23
The black glasshouse	24
Old Cat	25
Eldersville	26
Sorry, Mary	27
Stefni waiting	28
I've listened to you	29
Twenty blankets	30
One of their songs	31
Another one of their songs	32
What a piece of work is bird	33
I meet Harold McCarthy	34
They've gone	35
So I'm happy	36
How to get rid of a blowfly	37
O Freunde, nicht diese töne!	38
The garden chair and table set	39

Galahs ambulant	40
The vengeance of autumn	41
Kangaroo	42
2 Daddy meant happy	**43**
3 tall trees	**59**
The tree	61
Black Spur, Yarra Ranges	63
Undercrunch and birds	66
Seeds	68
Possums	70
Horn of plenty	74
Patriarchs	76
4 a man called Marlo	**79**
Marlo on the early train	81
Marlo and the war	83
Marlo and his daughter Emily	85
Marlo and his wife's flowers	88
Marlo and the Asian girl	90
Jessica	93
Marlo and the numbers	95
Marlo and the bowled dog	97
Sherry	100
Marlo and the dero	104
You make your own luck	107
Marlo visits old Ec	110
Old Ec on politics	113
Emily's day	116
Marlo dances with Kylie	118

1

paragraphs

Giant leap

So he's…my God he's standing. It works! A positive, an active sunlight flows through the wide picture window into the room. He does not know I'm here yet. I say his name softly. He turns around and sees me and all the atoms in the room vibrate. He outdoes the sun. I walk halfway towards him and he comes to meet me. He walks. He walks to me. I kneel. Even so, his face is well below mine. He giggles. The atoms in the room toggle out of control. Sunshine was made to light this scene. He is like a koala. Baby koala ball. Warm as if furred. Vertical at last, he walks the wide open plan room to find his mother. They come back beaming. We will never see him crawl again.

It's deep

How old were you that day? Very early years but walking well enough already with your chubby legs stretching into themselves and, beginning to talk, you would practise voice tones beyond your mother's or mine. Clearly it still comes to me, when the three of us walked over the rough splintery deck surrounding the tidal swimming pool – well upriver and black-brown muddy on the bank, rusty iron bars like prison gates to keep out the sharks, the water a dark dirty impenetrable green with me on high alert in case you fell. We watched as you peered down, perhaps seeking your reflection before you looked up and informed us, *Aaarrh…it's deep, it's deep,* with a slow side-to-side motion of the head and your voice long-drawn, sounding old and wise with the knowledge of many loose-timbered wharves and jetties and the cold green danger below them.

Supermarket monkeys

The woman behind me in the line at the supermarket toll gates is telling the one behind her how good her children are in the school holidays with the rain all week and how she reasons with them and they respond with real maturity so that, obviously, the two kids swinging Catherine wheels on the upright chrome pipe barrier between the toll gate aisles to try to loosen it from the bolts holding it to the floor and kicking me softly in the calves and sounding off more squealy loud and hoogly-hoogly than a troop of rare and endangered marmosets in a doco, could not possibly be hers.

Old men and little dogs

You see them a lot in this town – old men with little dogs. No longer roaming with Shep through meadows, well, paddocks. Up to the shops and back is enough. Across the traffic lights, pay the rates and two cans of beer at the pub will do these days for the open road and over the hills and far away. As they walk, the dog makes friends with everyone and allows the man in these last years to be the Earth, the centre of things. His dog is often white or whitish-grey like a little Moon, tethered to the man as the Moon is tethered to the Earth. Yes, it spins around him like the Moon, a little grey-white Moon dancing for him on its wagging tail.

Orange-bellied Parrot

The Tasmanian/Victorian orange-bellied parrot is prettier than a first girlfriend and almost extinct; seventy or so left in the wild. Then there's Hamas and Hezbollah and ISIS and Iraq (blood, bombs, rubble and dust) and Egypt and Syria and the Tamils, the Somalian pirates, the Sunnis and the Shiites not to mention Gaza and the concrete wall and the Palestinians and Israel (blood, bombs, rubble and dust)…who can keep up with it? The breeding program for the OBP has produced about 300 birds despite a very low rate of egg to fledgling survival. Millions of people subsist day after day, night after night in UN camps scattered throughout Africa; hungry, the babies crying all the time. The leading edge of the wing is enhanced by a magnetic, semi-iridescent dark blue.

Clawdette

Oh kitten, my kitten, my truelove, my kitten. She walks after me everywhere. Up the stairs. Down the stairs. The backyard. The bedroom. The toilet. The kitchen. A battery with legs and fur! Come on kitten. She is multihued in a subdued way. Subtle tones of browns, gingers and whites overlap, blend, intersect. At first I called her Coloured Cat, but as she grew, Clawdette! Rod McKuen wrote – love is giving what you need to get – a kind of pre-emptive trust. Perhaps it's just a practical thing. I give Clawdette what she needs so she'll give me what I need. She gives me what I need so she can get from me what she needs. But it's more than a contract. No boundaries can be measured between us and our nights have no complication.

Green gate

The saggy, scraping garden gate swings again thanks to moi! At first glance an agéd gate, heavy, with big wide pickets and an old fashioned semicircle arched top, part of the long Heritage Green fence along the side driveway. An easy job in the long run. All I had to do was move the hinge over a bit – three millimetres, just far enough to make new screw holes. Perpendicularity achieved and she swings again like a youngie. She don't swing both ways but – she's not that kind of girl. Only about 160 degrees back against the fence and no stumbling on the floor any more after I trimmed her base. Supple and free like a rock and roll dance girl unfurling out from me and skipping back in with a nice little kiss-click. My private, Heritage Green, rock-chick garden gate!

Heart of orange

OBP acknowledges his deficiencies. He admits the crimson rosella is brighter, more pleasing to look upon, like the best looking good kid in the class. He concedes the gang-gang has a handsome flair, an almost sinister bad-boy dark brooding quality. The rainbow is persistent, ingratiating, bossy; demands attention. OBP is quieter, less blatant, still waters. Yet he knows his worth; knows very few parrots can do anything with orange as well as he does. It's as if his heart has feather floated down to a different place and is asking you to work that little bit harder for him to find it.

Scabs

The Earth is an orange slowly succumbing to a fungus with powdery green scabs all over it. How to make the ugly truth poetic? What if you do? Run around proud and crowing, *Hey you all: look at my images, hear my subtle music?* YouTube shows Israelis cheering one of their rockets through the dark sky. The Palestinians do the same. Where's the poetry in that? Powdery green scabs, or human scabs, parch the rind. Bloody people. Fruitful, multiply, fill-the-Earth people exhaust its resources then move on to mutual mutilation. Next time you're communing with the grass, Mary Oliver, listen-feel for the little rumble-echoes of the bombs, succumb to the blissful odour of rocket exhaust.

Euroa green

The footpaths in Euroa are wide and most of them well mown. Wide. Level. Smooth. Green from March to December. A burnt brown, brittle khaki sort of colour through the worst of the summer. But, really, all jokes aside, to talk to your neighbour across the street takes planning. It's a long stroll over there. Maybe even take the car. Always – always – tell someone where you're going and when you think you'll be back. Euroa! Euroa! So many people know me by my name and half the time I've no idea who they are. Guess I'm a bit inward looking. Many of the streets have no kerb and gutter so the green just flows into a shallow scoop of a drain and out towards the bitumen like a ripple in a flicked blanket. It's pretty in a way. (I know – don't use 'pretty', 'nice', 'very' or 'got'!) And never any violence here. So much better than the Middle East you see on TV – all the blood, bombs, rubble and dust. How do people live like that?

Do they know

they are dying out? Is there a memory of the tribe being so much bigger? Do the older ones tell the younger ones how it used to be? The big swarms gathering together over the water in autumn and going back for spring and summer. The great muscle of numbers! The blue and green of the wings were flickering, flickering all over the sky. The air was a ripple-rumble of hundreds of little cacophonies. Do any people remember or have photographs of little orange domino dots on light green bodies flying overhead? Perhaps so many OBPs they blocked out the sun. Will they really, really stop being? The last four or five – what will they do? Sigh life away? What is a bird sigh? Think the others will be back soon? They're just over the hill – give a day or two and they'll be back. And even if they are conscious that it's futile, will they still set off in autumn because that's what they always do…

Scooter trains

What I'd like to see one day is a more orderly getting about on scooters by the olds. I want to see them form a scooter train like insects or caterpillars. The scooter captain doing a round up. Say, a 10 a.m. start and no excuses. The two most alert and responsible ones at the head and the tail: perhaps the younger olds, the still strong enough olds, do the guiding and the looking out for the frailer and less confident ones in between. Then off they go to the bowls or the men's shed or the crochet club or a stop outside the post office. They could work out a timetable. And when tragedy strikes, *The Gazette* could write up how *The close-knit Euroa scooter community was devastated today to learn of…*

Poetry requisites

A silent echo chamber. A quiet supermarket. They've forgotten the music. The loudspeakers are cold. Inconsequential noises fall into the air like the final few stones off a shovel. Footsteps. Tins and packets dropping into trolleys or baskets. Kids, suppressed by the silence, pad quietly, catlike, for a change. I stop singing to myself so as not to have some silly old duck say, *Someone sounds happy.* Hate that. Think of tombs, tombs with thick rock walls, a retail crypt, explosions in space at the movies without sound. Read the signs: cereals, marmalades, canned fruit, stationery, poetry requisites. No, I made the last one up. To do poetry requires little. You just have to be born with the virus and read a lot. No one with brains would seek to acquire it – this want or capability of seeing yourself in another person's words. You make poems by patiently, deliberately putting words together and hope others will see themselves in what you've made. I want it to be a mirror. People look in it, see themselves and if they like what they see the eyebrows will lift, the face seem to inflate.

The black glasshouse

My neighbour has erected a black glasshouse in his backyard. It is a large pyramid, five metres high. I suspect there has been no council approval. During the day it stabs the sky, trying to inject its black into the blue. It feels most at ease when night comes; in the womb again. The black panes seem translucent enough to filter in dark light so things that grow in caves will feel at home there. But so few plants grow in caves; it's mainly bats and worms. Perhaps his intentions are neither horticultural nor faunal but sculptural with its main functions (1) occupying and enhancing space and (2) making neighbours and visitors wonder? He may be secretly filming the different ways people have of scratching about their ears.

SBS Saturday 10.17 p.m.: *The Black Glasshouse* – an award-winning Swedish film about a gloomy family with secrets in a detached garage.

Old Cat

Handed in to the the RSPCA and then she became mine. Or I became hers. The smallest cat I've had but the one with the loudest purr. She was a well-aged tortoiseshell cat: amber, umber and a dash of white. Frail and bony when I brought her home, she was impossible to fatten. She wanted cuddles more than food. Couldn't think of a good name so I just called her The Old Cat. Through a friend who was too lazy to use all three words she became simply, Old Cat. I did my best to give her a golden sunset but I'd often wonder if she recalled her previous name and even heard it now and then in dreams. (They do appear to dream, don't they?) Maybe I would say the name without knowing it and spark her memories. Perhaps, after that, she'd yearn for 'Auld Lang Syne' and 'Yesterday'. Still, if the purring was anything to go by, she seemed happy enough just being Old Cat.

Eldersville

I called in to see her in Eldersville. She wasn't happy. *I don't know why I can't be at home. I've got the neighbours. They call in every day.* Obviously the doctor is worried if you fall or have some kind of accident, I offered. I knew it wouldn't be well received; she'd been through all the pros and cons. *I'm the bloody liveliest one here. Look at this room: it's more a cell than a room. And Grey Girl needs me. Did you see Grey Girl?* I told her I'd seen Grey Girl and had a long talk with her before she skulked off under the house. *Anyhow Wayne's coming down on Friday to talk to the doctors again; try and straighten them out. Matron keeps dragging me into the activities room. Cards and knitting and bloody Scrabble. You know what I call it?* I said that I didn't and laughed expecting something funny. She said, *I call it the departure lounge.*

Sorry, Mary

I was a bit hard on Mary Oliver back in 'Scabs'. She has a delightful poem, 'Just lying on the grass at Blackwater', where she's in the grass feeling all connected and full of wonder. Flowers in the toes, wish I was a parrot: that sort of stuff. I like that kind of poem. A couple of Australian poets, Mark O'Connor and Andrew Lansdown, also write movingly on the blood-sap connection. It's just that when I read them my mind always drifts away to the screen, to blood, bombs, rubble and dust and those dry shattered lands and twenty of God's children huddled in a room with a big bottle of water-from-the-well in the corner. I think of Yeats and that rough beast slouching towards Bethlehem. No longer slouching. Not towards. There. Upright. Sharp claws. Howling fire from the sky. Look up Mary Oliver's 'The Snakes'. Awesome little packet of words. Wish I could write one that good.

Stefni waiting

Stefni was heartbroken and it's hard for a father when I see that and know there is nothing I can do about it. She's camped in her old cream Kombi at the cove where the birds spend summer each year. She's been there about four weeks now, just waiting, watching and increasingly despairing they'll return. She'd always been in love with birds. Did her doctorate on migration – there's a lot more of it in Australia than people know about. She rings her mother and me every night. *They're not coming back, Dad.* What could we say? We knew it was on the cards, more likely than not. She'd always been such an optimistic little thing, always looking forward. I remember once when we were visiting relatives in Melbourne for Moomba her uncle asked her, *How old are you now, Steff?* and she replied, *Fourteen next January. And please, Uncle, can you call me Stefni. I hate being called Steff.* It's hard for her to be optimistic these days. *I'll stay another week, Dad. You never know.*

I've listened to you

So after I'd explained everything in really simple terms for him he looked at me coldly and said, *I've listened to you, now you listen to me.* Well, what would be the point? I'd already stated my position. I've considered all the yeas and nays of the situation and the simple fact is – he's wrong. He obviously wasn't paying a lot of attention to what I'd been saying or he wouldn't have come up with this self congratulating, belligerent stance. Although, I did like the rhetorical balance in his way of expressing it. I found it reminded me of Dickens – best of times…worst of times; far, far better thing…far, far better rest; listened to you…listen to me. I reckon Charles himself could have come up with it. Anyway, when he'd finished I asserted, in a warm voice tone completely opposite to his, *If you'd listened to me in the first place you would know my feelings on the matter are fact-based and there is no chance of them changing.* Some people find it hard to admit it when they're wrong. Have you noticed that?

Twenty blankets

It was one of those things you get and when you tell people about it they say, *Yeah, it's going around.* The headache, the loss of balance, the clogged nose, the general sense of being heavy, of just wanting to crawl into your bed and pile twenty blankets over you. People tell you, *Oh, I had that. It took weeks to go. Does it make you feel tired and negative and depressed?* The way they describe the symptoms doesn't make you feel any better. Mainly it makes you want to go out and buy, or steal, blankets. Nothing works to relieve it. Just a waste of money to buy Codrals or even Aspros. Amid all the generalised what's-the-point-of-it-all-I'm-a-total-failure-and-may-as-well-leave-the-planet-anyway feelings there seems no silver lining. A man my age should have granddaughters to look after him when something like this happens; good strong optimistic young girls halfway into their pharmacy degrees. They'd know what to give me. Something under the counter. Failing that – blankets, twenty blankets. *Le cocon impénétrable.*

One of their songs

So that's the graph and it shows the results of our surveys over the last year or so. Surprisingly this sound pattern (they call a repeated sound pattern a 'song' or more generally 'music') recurs fairly regularly every seventh day. The culture we're studying call this day Saturday. This particular song is played usually without words and you'll see there are favoured times, usually around three o'clock in the afternoon: sometimes a little earlier, sometimes a little later. I'll play it for you. Note the rising sensation in the music; the sense of firmness and hope it conveys. We have studied their septal regions and, believe me, without exception this kind of tone in the music does produce a very pleasant excitation. The words are often not sung but would translate roughly as a female person is approaching and is about to be permanently united with a male person.

Another one of their songs

One of their more interesting songs is played sporadically almost everywhere. Indeed from what we can gather this one is almost like a universal background hum of noise across the planet. Barely a minute goes by without we pick it up somewhere. It is far more sombre, or solemn than the one about the female person approaching. It features one of their common words – a heavy stress on the first syllable, much lighter on the second and then heavy again on the third as if that last syllable was trying to get back the strength of the first but can't quite make it. In contrast to the woman-approaching-us song this one is often played at funerals. Perhaps they sum up two of the prominent feelings of these people – their hope and their sadness. It translates as something like: the day before the current one.

What a piece of work is bird

In eyesight how ingenious; this way, that way, all around; sharply focused and far-seeing; and such expanded capabilities for kinds of light we cannot see. In claws how perfect for each purpose; talons for grabbing and ripping, tightening circlets for holding on, paddles for swimming. In territorial conflict religiously intense. In voice so melodious, chattering, symphonic. And what of the hollow flute-like bones; so practical for keeping in the air. In form and moving how musical; how swift when needed, how calm and slow as required. Circling up, up in perfect concord with the facts of physics. And well-designed enough to fly under water! In companionship how trusting; in the hand how warm; on the fingers so light. And the multifunction feathers so waterproofing, such insulation, such flirtatious display and so useful for flying! What a piece of work! In navigation miraculous. In breeding patterns so hard, so on the edge of impossible, so almost obtuse and perverse in their difficulties. Quintessence of living dust. Bird delights me.

I meet Harold McCarthy

Harold, Harold McCarthy. People call me Roland. Finally a very long overdue introduction with my neighbour! I praise myself for the straight face when I said, *David, David Kelly. Call me David. That's an interesting piece of garden adornment,* I suggested, nodding towards the black glass pyramid in the middle of his yard. *Is it for meditation – sort of black Zen? Or does it make the plants grow dark green leaves?* I could see he was getting a little unhappy at my line of attack. *I'm being serious – there are all sorts of plants. It could be an aerial or something. Egyptian sort of thing.* His silence was eloquent, as they say. *Well, I've been here about four years now and I thought it wrong somehow that we had never exchanged names. Looks like something from the Mother Ship*, I said. *Yes*, he replied, *yes, we use it to help amplify sound waves, radio transmissions and so on...*

SBS Saturday 10.17 p.m.: *The Black Glasshouse* – an award-winning Swedish film about a gloomy family with secrets in a detached garage.

They've gone

There are thousands of holes in the sky they used to fly through. A big flock wheeling like an Andromeda. Maybe they spun around in a Fibonacci spiral. I bet they did! I bet if we could get a film of them circling and expanding – perning in a gyre as Yeats would say – you could find Fibonacci magic in it. Too late now: they've gone, bar the ones in cages, and OBPs don't breed well in cages. If you hang around the bays they used to frequent you'll hear them in the grasses. You'll see the tall pale grasses bending over with their weight and springing to vertical again when they hop down to the ground. And something will be waiting there – a devil, a feral cat, a goanna perhaps with all senses on high hunger. Maybe a man or a woman with a camera and tape recorder will be there too. Back in the study they can scan over and over all night but they'll never see the pixels, they'll never hear the resonance of the OBP as it flew off the wind-brushed grass that day. The holes in the sky they used to fly through are shrinking and filling in.

So I'm happy

I'm walking along the street, any street. I'm feeling very *hello lamp post how yer going?* I'm probably whistling. I might be singing to myself. I'm at peace with the world. I've forgiven myself and all my debtors and, indeed, my creditors. I understand why I didn't become what I wanted to become. I'm sure many of you have been there. Then my pleasant little moment is interrupted by some old duck in her seventies. *Someone sounds happy,* she'll say. It instantly snaps the mood. She looks at me and grins something mischievous, something superior, something almost malicious. It's like she's saying, *I've found you out – you're happy. Go on, admit it.* And I have to smile back and I do BUT I really feel like saying, *So what? So I'm happy. What's the big deal? What's it got to do with you? Can't a man be happy in this town for a few small minutes without some silly old moo remarking on it and giggling? Eff off!*

How to get rid of a blowfly

There is the vulgar way. Aerosol. Flyspray. Poison the bloody thing. Kill it. After all it has no right, none whatsoever, to enter my/your house and buzz forever. Who owneth the house maketh the rules. Right? Right! But you, like me, are not vulgar. I'll tell you how I did it. Set the scene. Sunday night between nine and ten. Resting, stretched out on the bed but I have left the light on in the room where the poetry desk is. Fly buzzing all around that room and the light. Thinks to myself – it will grow tired, run out of energy and keel over and fall asleep. No way. This fly's on pills. So I finally decide to do something about it. Out I go. Turn on the light in a room closer to the back door than the poetry room. Turn off the light in the poetry room. Next step: turn on the back veranda light. Turn off the light of the in-between room. You see the pattern. Get the picture. Fly goes to back veranda. I quickly close the door. No fly. Quietness reigns. I tell you: if you really want something in this life – really want it – you can get it. You don't have to be vulgar – you don't – but you do have to be clever.

O Freunde, nicht diese töne!

When I read about space and how big it is; how much of it is out there; how we try to visualise it as an ever expanding balloon but without a skin it just seems too big a problem. How did it happen? Anyhow, I was thinking that one day a couple of hundred years ago God was looking down and watching us as we try to figure it out with physics – reasonless causal physics – and he was laughing at us and our puny small-beer minds. Also, he was becoming irritated, almost to the point of offence, that some people really didn't think he was. No God. Full stop. End of story. He knew he was, that he is, that he always will be, but he could see that the believers were having a lot of trouble convincing the stellar curious. So he thought, I will cause something to come from nothing that will be so undeniably excellent people will have to know it could have only come from me. I'll make Beethoven. His ninth symphony will be all the proof they'll ever need.

The garden chair and table set

The old lightweight metal set of four chairs and a small circle-top table is still intact. There are no broken pieces. It all sits level and secure. The problem is that the paintwork has been knocked about over the years. A few cheap spray cans and Robert's your uncle! The job is easy, although a bit tedious and the thin coat of sprayed black is very light on the bare patches of metal. Still, a second spray and a third selective spray has got them looking like they were…resprayed. But is it art? Could be – going by the things you see in art galleries these days! A pile of bricks. A dozen grey stones with a cockatoo feather on each one. A slew of old fence palings thrown down like fiddlesticks. A room with marbles all over the floor. Why not these four chairs akimbo around the small circle-top table with five or six spray cans and their removed lids all sprinkled around a large mat of artificial grass with random black spray patches on it? Why not?

Galahs ambulant

Two galahs are ambulating quickly over a wide expanse of concrete footpath. Their claws were not designed for flat hard concrete: much more useful on branches or grassy bumpy ground. Their feet are four-pronged, all-terrain, ambulatory prehensile engineering marvels! They rock side to side a bit like two old crocks with stones in their shoes but there flows from their comical walking something musical as well. They are avoiding people. Not only myself but also a talking group of four that has intruded on their pecking space. So they take flight. Well, not flight. They take walk. They take pink and grey galah quick waddle-walk. They are silent but look at each other for reassurance or perhaps confirmation that the threat from the tall two-legs doesn't warrant the expense of wing energy. Not yet. Might if they get closer. But for now they amble.

The vengeance of autumn

First sign's a little coldness in the toes at night. Then there's thinking soup instead of salad. Trees looking a little unhappy and going yellow at the leaf tips. The cricket's over. The football rams up. The cats begin to come in a little earlier. The weather less and less predictable. Will it rain? What of the wind? Snow this weekend on the highest peaks. Perhaps it's time to put the heater on, perhaps not. Are the hot water bottles still sound? New flannelette sheets? With summer on the wane, the days were very liveable. You began to think that you were in control. Sucked in! For now autumn makes you work to warm up a bit. My neighbour streams out crocodile tears about the grandchildren staying over Easter. Glad when it's over. Sure! Is ANZAC a Monday or a Friday this year? Then there's the daylight saving change-back. Autumn makes you reassess the humdrum day to day of living. While the vengeance of autumn may seem subtle, when it clicks its fingers you'll find yourself asking, *How high?*

Kangaroo

I stop the car to look at the kangaroo in the flat dry paddock. Presenting a three-quarter best face with alert donkey stiff ears, it looks back at me. An hour to sunset and the bright harshness of this day, halfway through the summer, is paling. The grass is that bronze khaki colour as hard to describe as the indefinite vowel at the end of words such as wire: a tone brittle and soft at the same time. The grass is still long enough to agitate slightly in occasional lazy wind puffs. The kangaroo is alone although I know there is a small mob that hovers around this farm. The one I'm watching is a large animal, probably male and he dominates my focus. He stands in and bisects his own horizon. The blurry quality of his light grey fur blends in with the fuzzy grass. He seems at ease, meant to be there, curvy, both fluid and solid at the same time, as if drawn up from the bed rock to stand above the jittery pasture, moulded and shaped by the invisible fingers of a master sculptor.

2

Daddy meant happy

1.

daddy meant happy
that was one of the first things I knew
daddy wasn't there all day
daddy went early and came back
at the end of the day before dark
daddy used to throw me in the air
towards the green ceiling
a little scared but laughing
mummy was cooking
and when daddy came home
he'd come into the room
where mummy was cooking
and he'd pick me up
and throw me high
and he'd always catch me
and I'd always laugh
and mummy would laugh
and daddy meant happy

2.

sometimes I'd look through the window
and if I moved my head from side to side
or closer and away from the window
the grass and the path
would be all wavy
like a kicked up carpet
although it was really flat
but if it could be wavy
as I could make it look
I could run a truck
up and down
over the bumps all day

3.

the birds must have shops too
somewhere in trees and bushes
somewhere else
where the trees are bigger
they must have shops to get their food
just like we do up the street

4.

we're on the veranda
and mummy's knitting
she's sitting in granny's
old yellow cane chair knitting
and we're watching the rain
on the other side of the street for a long time
we're dry over here but over there
god's watering the houses
to make them grow
slowly it comes over to our side
and we start getting wet
bits of water like
hundreds and thousands
so we go back inside the house
and close the doors to the veranda
and go down the hall
and set ourselves up in the lounge room
and mummy switches on
the little round fire

5.

I'm in the backyard with daddy
and he wants a match
tells me to go and ask mummy for a match
I'm not allowed to play with matches
have to leave them alone
have to go and ask mummy for a match
but mummy's not there
and I know where the matchbox is
and I'm grown-up now anyway
so I open the box and take out two matches
and take them out to daddy
two in case one doesn't work
or maybe he wants two
and he laughs but I don't get into trouble

6.

uncle Bill comes one Saturday
we've got two uncle Bills
this is not the one that goes to America
I know there's something wrong
with this uncle Bill
I just feel it the way they're all talking
quietly together
it's grown-ups talking
about things we wouldn't understand
he asks if I want an ice cream
of course I do
so he gives me money
a lot of money
and I say must be a big ice cream
and he smiles and says yeah
so my big brother takes me up the street
to get the ice cream
and we come back with a cone each
and they laugh and I realise
we were supposed to get a brick

7.

I don't want to have to sleep
in the room with my brother
I want to sleep with mummy and daddy
the cot was better
the bed's too big
and my brother's not so good
one night I go back into the big bedroom
where mummy and daddy sleep
and crawl over daddy and get between them
like I used to and daddy wakes up
quickly and grabs me
daddy seems scared
but I know as soon as he knows it's me
it'll be all right
and mummy says let him stay
but daddy says no
and takes me back to the other room

8.

mummy seems happy
when I want to look
at the encyclopaedias
but makes me wash my hands
then brings them out from the sideboard
it's made of black wood and has curved doors
she lays them on the table
and opens them for me and I sit
at the kitchen table looking through them
although I can't read
the pictures are good
and the paper is soft and shiny
and every now and again
there's a colour picture
I like those more
than the black and white ones
there are two books
brown covers with gold writing
I'm not sure how long we do it for
but after a while we stop
and she puts them away
we do it again sometimes
I like touching them
and opening them

9.

they tell me that
tomorrow
someone's coming
to take the cat away
but I like the cat and won't let them
I take her into the bathroom
and close the door
she's a nice colour
like an orangey brown
she's soft and warm
makes a nice noise
and she doesn't do anything wrong
she always lets me touch her
and I tell her that she
can always stay with us
and I hold her a lot
but then the man comes
and there's nothing I can do
he's smiling at the front door
and takes her away
not just mummy's fault
daddy could have stopped it

10.

before I go to bed mummy or daddy
take me outside the front door
it's dark and I don't want to be
out there by myself but
it's OK with them around
and daddy holds me up
and I reach out my hand
and catch a star
sometimes I just leave it out
and wait for the star to fall into it
and daddy says have you got one yet
and I say yeah or sometimes
I'll say no it fell through my fingers
and wave my hand around
until I catch another one
then they carry me back in
and put me to bed
and daddy rubs his hand
over my ears and my hair

11.

good thing about being sick
with the mumps
is they make a fuss over me
and I get presents
this time a tram conductor's
ticket set so I take out
the middle cushion of the lounge
and it's like tram seats
and although I don't have the purply black
uniform and cap I can walk
around my tram and get off
and get on the long step
like the conductor can
but I'm beginning to run out
of the one-penny tickets

12.

why are there spiders
if they're going to bite you
as mummy keeps telling me
but one day on the grass
I saw one and told daddy
there's a spider
and he said not to worry
and smiled at me
and let it run over his hand

13.

Ticki wouldn't wake up
her shiny black body was floppy
my brother didn't know what was going on
we put some food in front of her
but she wouldn't eat it
as soon as mummy came home
we showed her
and when daddy came in
he took Ticki to the vet
I wasn't allowed to go
had to wait at home
daddy came back without her
a bait   thallium   probably
from the fish and chip shop
across the back fence a few doors down
we don't go there any more
start going to the other one
although it's a long way up the street
I always sing that song
'Cindy Oh Cindy'
as *Ticki Oh Ticki*

3

tall trees

The tree

As trees go the mountain ash
are at the higher and thicker end:
after two or three centuries
up to more than a hundred metres.
They'll grow taller than a SpaceX.
They can be three metres at the base
and even way, way up they can still be
more than a metre through the trunk.
The branches which, from the ground
appear thin and scrawny
like the arms of witches,
don't start until maybe halfway
or even two thirds of the way
to the top and then they twist
out and curl around reaching
upwards like they're trying
to tie themselves in knots.
You'll see long thin streamers
of bark dangling in the wind
where the branches join the trunk
and from the base a thick rough
bandage of brown wraps the trunk
for three or four times the height
of a man or a tall woman.
Beyond that, the bark
which was smooth and white
when the tree was young
has become with age a dirty cream,
pitted and grubby and stained.

If you look closely up there
up seventy or eighty metres,
ninety or a hundred if you're lucky,
you will slowly pick out
little fissures and tree cave openings
where spiders, lizards, crickets,
moths, beetles, long crawlies
with hundreds of legs,
many kinds of possums and gliders
and bird after bird scratch
their nest holes deeper and deeper
into this big living block of flats.

And here's the sad thing:
all this animal frenzy
of renovation and extension
and additions is letting in
the water and termites
that will eventually rot
this big block of flats
right out from under them
or from their offspring
rippling down another
hundred years or so.
Unfair for sure, but all this clamour
of life invited in and nurtured
by the generosity of this tree
is one of the things
that will finally bring it down.

Black Spur, Yarra Ranges

Along the Black Spur road
out of Healesville
there is a forest of them
put in by hand in the 1940s
after two huge bushfires.
It's like a plantation,
a garden of tall organ flutes
with an under-ruffle of ferns.
Mind blowing to look at
but there are few other trees
in that setting and it's not
the way they do it themselves.
Left to their own devices
these high sky yearners,
Eucalyptus regnans,
make forests of eery complexity
with different middle storey trees,
lower storey shrubs and ground plants
depending on the rain,
the side of the hill and so on.

If it's really wet on a south-east
mountain side a true rainforest
evolves with lichen-overed
myrtle beech and sassafras
and once they get their roots in
and their leaves out
those leaves will keep the sun
off the ground so far below
that the mist and the fog
will hang in the air all day
so it's almost always
gripping wet and gloomy:
a dark magic elves green.
On the ground you'll find
ferns and mosses and fungi.
Things like worms and slugs
that love damp and cool
and squelch and slime
are in their element
and thrive down there.

But where they're facing
west and north, exposed
to drier winds and more sun,
silver wattle and blackwood
are more prominent.
You'll still get the ferns
but a more prickly undercrunch.

All this morphs and changes
as you go up and over ridges
then down into the gullies
and up and out again:
after a while anyone can
start to pick out the changes.

These big trees don't like
growing too close to each other.
The scientists call them *crown shy.*
They prefer to spread out a bit
and let other plants grow in between.
Once they're up high enough
they'll look over the forest
like ministers in green robes,
bending and creaking with the wind,
giving off a noise that could be
a loud hum and a soft roar in one.

They inspire hundreds of things
to live in, on and around them.
They do so much they could brag about
but like the truly elevated
they're always modest
with a soft strong voice.

Undercrunch and birds

Down in the undercrunch
is where it all begins.
So much more goes on down there
than we can ever see:
leaves and strips of bark,
the hard and soft droppings
of parrots and honeyeaters,
of lizards, snakes and possums;
the shed skin, fallen feathers,
decaying skeletons,
the bodies of boneless snails
and always the water dripping down,
seeping down into that
rich brown undercrunch
that the forest makes of itself
to make itself.

Birds complete the forest
like ornaments in a room
with their colour, sound and flash
against all that brown and green.
The birds add tangerine and scarlet,
iridescent purples and blues,
chartreuse, yellow, orange, lime:
every colour in the dictionary.
When they die they add
the stored up goodness of their bodies
and when their eggs hatch
and the shells are discarded
it all goes into the undercrunch.

Day and night they add
all sorts of sounds.
There's always at least
one of them somewhere
twittering, hooting, boo-hooing,
belling, cawing, singing
something or other
to some other bird
that's answering back.
They swerve through the forest
like atoms trailing flashes of colour,
like little comets or shooting stars:
and they carry seeds everywhere
helping to spread the forest
and keep it varied.
Of course the lyrebird,
head-down-tail-up eccentric,
is always pottering in its larder garden,
raking up the undercrunch,
helping to keep it exposed,
turning it over and breaking it down
making that rich brown yeast.

The trees and the smaller plants,
all the mosses and fungi,
the bugs and spiders and birds
and the possums and the wombats –
the whole lot's made from the interaction
of sunlight, water, air and undercrunch.
Everything comes from it.
Everything goes back to it.

Seeds

All seeds take their chance.
All things want to grow up
to be what they're meant to be
and so they push and stretch themselves.

Something inside says, *Go down.*
So roots go down where other roots
have gone, gaining strength
through the soft brown undercrunch
to push into the harder clay and rock below
saying, *I'll go in here now.*
This dark space is mine now.
Though the crowns of these trees are shy
their roots are sociable.
Their pubs are the cavernous aquifers
where their flimsy root filaments
feel each other out with secret handshakes;
an immense under-nation
holding onto each other,
supporting each other
in ways we'll never understand.

Something else inside says, *Rise.*
And slowly a soft green question mark
feels its way up through the air,
yearning for straight,
yearning for high
and as years roll in
and years roll out
becomes harder and stronger,
becomes bole and trunk,
then divides out to branches,
divides out to leaves and flowers
whispering to all the others,
I have come to join you.
I belong up here with you now.

Possums

Possums are eaten by powerful owls
and I'm not sure I would have
put those owls in the big trees
had I been around that first week.

Then again, even though possums
are slow breeders,
if they weren't cut back a bit
they'd soon overrun the joint
and eat out their food supplies
so maybe there has to be
something there to keep them down.

Every night as the sun goes down
the big trees shake out their possums.
You could set your watch by it.

There is no typical or average possum.
They adapt and evolve to living
in many different places
and will change their diet
to what's available. Some
have developed very strict ways
of getting their food and breeding.
The little ringtails make a nest
of intertwined twigs and leaves
like a hollowed out AFL ball.
Others, such as the leadbeaters
and the mountain brushtails
and gliders live in holes
in the older mountain ash trees.

You'll often see a possum sitting
fairly still for a long time.
It may be rocking back and forth
like a cat listening to music
but it's actually digesting
because some of the leaves and sap
that possums eat are quite toxic
and they rest between eating bouts
to give their stomachs time
to absorb and process it all.

Throughout the night
they do the usual animal things:
lick each other, fight each other,
glare at each other,
raise their ears, raise their voices,
swish their fluffed-out tails,
leave their scent marks.
And there's not just one
possum lifestyle.
Each type has its own social life,
its own diet and child rearing ways.
The yellow-bellied gliders
are patriarchal with a dominant male
and up to five females or juveniles
snuggled in the one nest.

The leadbeaters are matriarchal
and often sleep up to eight or ten in a nest,
the breeding pair and their offspring
and maybe an unmarried uncle or two
but only the one adult female.
She'll drive her daughters away
a good half year earlier than her sons,
forcing them to make their own families.
They eat moths and tree crickets
and use their claws and teeth
to scratch into the bark
and suck the sap from the ash trees
and the trees in the understorey,
but they don't eat leaves or fruit or flowers
as much as the other possums.

For about fifty years
it was thought they'd died out
before they were rediscovered
in the nineteen sixties.
Brushtails and gliders also nest
in the ash trees but hardly ever
eat insects and spiders.
They're mainly gatherers
while the leadbeaters are both
hunters and gatherers.

There are so few left and so many
threats to their survival
that rough times lie ahead for them.
Due to all the logging
and the bushfires
in around 50 years or so
most of the old dead trees
the leadbeaters nest in
will have rotted through
and crashed to the forest floor
while the younger trees
will not have grown old enough
to form the hollows they need
to nest in. There'll be many years,
decades in fact, when the holes
these possums need for their
home-sweet-home will be fewer
and farther between.

Horn of plenty

The protest about cutting down
old-growth forests comes from
the fact that birds and animals
need a mix of trees and shrubs,
ground, middle and high storey
for all their complex needs
and when we restart a forest
with just one kind of tree
many of the animals and birds
that used to thrive in that area
can't come back to it because
there are neither nesting sites
nor the kinds of food they need.
The trees and shrubs also need
the whole range of animals
and insects to keep them growing.
After we've cut down
the old-growth forests
we can't just put a few seeds in
and expect them back in fifty years:
with the best will in the world
we can never make it
the way it used to be.

But natural death in the forest
is far from final.
It often means increase not decrease:
big old ash trees full of termites
and possum holes and water rot,
mud-gut they call it,
will finally crash one day
back to the undercrunch
they came from 400 years before
and straight away
in any gash of sunlight
things start growing:
fungi and flowers that insects
and spiders and birds will eat:
and a seed will float down
from the living trees
and lodge in some tiny crevice
in that fallen log and start to grow
feeding off its slow decay:
other plants will respond
to the sunlight that now streaks
into the gloomy undercrunch.
It could make you believe in
spontaneous generation
the way that iridescent tomb
gets rammed full of life.

Patriarchs

Centuries down the track
if we leave that seed alone
and it grows in the right soil
and the right side of the hill
it might be another Ada or Furmston tree:
three metres across at the ground,
forty people posing in front of it
or a giggle of tree huggers
holding hands at its base.

And the possums and gliders
will be eating all night
and the birds and lizards
will be eating all day
but that tree will be eating
and drinking all day and all night
for three or four hundred years,
breathing air through its leaves,
eating dirt from deep down,
drinking in the mist and fog
through its high leaves –
the mist and fog that keeps
the sun away and keeps the rain in
so water soaks to the deepest roots.

Forest guardians. Green elders,
creaking and humming
their windy sermons,
they will rent out their rooms
to bugs and birds and spiders
and possums and frogs
for hundreds of years.
Trees are unique among
the planet's living things:
for themselves they take
only air, water and dirt
but make life possible
for everything that comes
near them.

    Tree means give.

4

a man called Marlo

Marlo on the early train

On the early train,
halfway to the city, Marlo
is feeling squashed.
He puts another crease in *The Age*
and tries hard to keep the freehold
he had staked for himself
on the boxy seat half an hour back.
Bloody fat people, he thinks.

It's been twenty-five years now that
Marlo's taken the 6.38.
Once upon a time it was quiet enough
to read the main bits,
even get some work out of the way
writing by hand. No laptops!
He'd be at the desk by 7.30
and Light Brigading his day
before the first calls.

Now you may as well origami
the bloody paper as try to read it.
Mr Elbows here
is clearly into expansion.
Marlo can't stand big passengers,
the way they shuffle and spread
and now with the new city
interchange at Westerville
and the timetable changes
there are more of them
and the trip's eight minutes longer.
Lately he's been thinking of the 6.19.

Everything's louder
in the city loop.
The dark crush of people
reflects in the window
like a grey forest of bamboo.
He notes his frown:
how the years have slashed
more channels in it.
On his briefcase he can
at least smooth the paper out.
Finished with it? from Mr Elbows.
Marlo puts *The Age* in his briefcase,
stands wordless,
shoulders his way off the train.

Marlo and the war

The war was really getting to Marlo
and he could hardly work all week.

For the last few days
his secretary, Leanne,
had noticed he was out of sorts.

On Thursday he left the office
for an early lunch
and found himself drifting into
A and Rs for something on the war:
His eyes rested upon
Why they need us there.
Hopefully it would answer all his questions.

Then it was up to Staves
for that innovative Massenet cantata
he'd seen reviewed in *The Age*
and – what had Leanne suggested? –
some new herbal tea,
Sargisi, or something similar, that
she'd found at The Yeti's Shawl.
While there he couldn't resist
a pair of soft Tibetan slippers.
What the hell – treat myself, he thought.

Marlo returned to the office
with all his presents and his mind
in turmoil over the war.
He asked Leanne to make up the Sargisi.
Then when she returned from lunch
he asked her to hold his calls,
The old lie please Leanne – in conference.
He thanked her for the Sargisi
and to the rapid tinkle of the teaspoon
he'd fumble his feet frequently
in and out of the new Tibetan slippers
while, with the Massenet playing quietly,
he gleaned *Why they need us there*
for its ore of lies and half lies and shock.

Occasionally he'd hear the phone ring
and Leanne picking it up quickly
so he wouldn't be disturbed,
her soft girl's voice calling
out to him who it had been
all the long afternoon
as he read about the war.

Marlo and his daughter Emily

From the earliest days
Emily had been more secretive,
not telling them things,
more inclined to play alone,
not bringing herself forward
like the other two.
And she hadn't slept well,
always harder getting her to sleep
than her older and younger sisters.

Not surprising she'd be the one
to leave home first.
He'd always suspected
she'd made the plan early.
It seemed she'd already left them
a long, long time ago,
even though she had stayed
living with them until sixteen,
using them like a cat would
and then leaving like a cat would.

One of the attractions for her
of nursing was that she could live in
at the nurses' quarters;
and then she'd moved to Brisbane
and the contact stopped.

He and Jill looked for reasons,
looked for early clues
that would seem to predict it
as if by going back
and doing something different,
responding differently to that early sign
they could have changed the course.

He'd chosen Leanne for his secretary
because she reminded him of Emily
but for all that Leanne
is so much happier in herself
and eager to help and share.

It was always hard to get Emily
to do anything around the house;
hard enough with kids
but it shouldn't be.

So hard. Especially on Jill.
A secretive resentful daughter
can break anyone's heart.
Their eldest, Antonia,
and their youngest, Kylie,
were always helpful, happy girls.
Worst thing: neither he nor Jill knew
why Emily was so hard on them,
why she so wanted to keep them away.

Had they, had he perhaps,
taught her to dislike herself
or was it someone she met one night
in dark air down a flight of stairs
– red lights – loud sounds – long drinks:
some damned smiling
drug fucked drongo
who turned her against them?

But, no. That wasn't it.
The turn had been festering for years.

He knows when he looks in a mirror
there is something missing in his face,
not just the ageing,
something that was there
while she was still at home.
Whatever it was it is not there now.
It might come back if she returns.

Marlo and his wife's flowers

Today is a flowers day.

As each year starts
Marlo will open his diary
at five random pages
and write in *flowers*.
On those days
he will take home
a bunch of flowers for Jill.

So, after leaving the office
as usual for the 4.11
he made the same mistake
he did last time.
He bought the flowers
from that old woman
with the helium gas voice:
Been naughty, have we?

He hates her empty laugh,
the silly embracing smile.
He thinks of coins
rattling in a Sally's can.

At last the train pulls in.
He finds a seat but starts
to feel self-conscious trying
to keep his briefcase steady,
finish reading *The Age*
and protect the flowers
all at the same time.

Getting back in the good books?

This from something old
on rubber legs
rocking like a wave in the aisle
beside his seat.
He folds *The Age*
into his briefcase
and offers the seat.

I'll hold 'em for ya if ya like.

Marlo ignores her,
tries to balance,
loses it,
grabs the back of the seat.
A fat girl sitting opposite
joins rubber legs
in a conspiracy of giggles.

Jellies on train seats,
he thinks and feels his fingers
almost crush the flowers.
He slinks away towards
the doors of the carriage,
three more stations…
He repeats it like a prayer,
three more stations…

Marlo and the Asian girl

Some weeks later Marlo
was on the train engrossed
in his second book on the war,
How many's too many?
when a young Asian girl,
maybe twenty,
willowed in
and sat beside him.

Slim, dark-haired,
wearing a bright tight
silky red and gold
Chinese dress.
A walking flower,
he thought.
She'd no sooner
sunk into the seat than,
all at once,
her head lolled
onto his shoulder
like a friendly ghost
and she fell asleep.

He could think of no
recent act of generosity
to deserve this.

To wake her
meant touching her
and he couldn't do that,
yet to leave her there
was so obviously wrong.

His mind looking for a lifeline
fixed his eyes on the elderly woman,
he guessed in her seventies,
sitting opposite.

He smiled weakly:
What do I do?
She smiled back,
I don't know.

He felt himself flushing
into red face.

At the next station,
as the train slowed,
China sort of hinged
away from him
and back against him
as if she wanted to keep
going with the train.

She woke into a soft
self-effacing panic,
a small laugh.
Sorry, she blurted
and bolted.

Marlo sighed out his relief,
exchanged a smile-laugh
with the old lady.

Then after the train
rattled up again
he closed the book on the war
and shut his eyes
and indulged himself
drawing out
the memory of
how it had felt to have
her young warm body
seeping into his arm
and onto his shoulder.

He wondered, maybe, perhaps,
he'd actually fallen asleep
for a station or two
and had been dreaming.

Jessica

Hardly slept last night up till 4 with the essay
then Glasi came in at 6 so I had to get up
and listen to her
and then the classes this morning

The boyfriend leaned forward
and painted her with his eyes.

so it wasn't until about three
that I got home and there was this box
on the veranda
and the phone before I could open it
and the text messages
there's a lot to attend to in an A student's day
anyway the gift-wrapped box on the veranda

The boyfriend tried to look impassive,
resisting a great urge to hold her hand
and stroke her face.

with instructions time and coordinates
where and 'wear' as it were
anyhow you'll never guess
what happened on the train
I sat down beside this old flabby thin hair
and I must have fallen asleep
I woke at the next stop and realised
my head was flopped over on his shoulder
I zipped off bloody quick and caught the next train
he was so obviously Liberal
a pretentious old shit
so that's why I'm late and I'm glad you waited

The boyfriend kept smiling.

no one's given me anything like this before
I mean I've had cheongsams before
but not given
not given like this
not like you give

Their eyes locked more tightly
and the boyfriend stroked her face.

no one's ever stroked my face like you do

Marlo and the numbers

Numbers had always
flitted around Marlo's head.
He'd picked them up early.
He could out-multiply
most of the kids in the street,
came second in the big maths test
at the end of primary school.
(The winning kid's dad was a teacher.)

When he first heard
of the Fibonacci numbers
the name suggested
witchcraft, mysticism
or the dark arts.
At the very least something exotic
beyond explaining the layout of seeds
in a sunflower:
an exponential growth
more stately and subtle
than easy doubling.
*Classical music compared
to pop,* said one of his teachers.

On any given day Emily
recedes further from him,
more away than yesterday
and the day before combined.

Infinity bothered him a lot
when he was younger.
It had been hard to wrap his mind
around the idea of *still-one-more*
as a perpetual condition,
the concept of something
that never ever ends.
If the universe were infinite
and the stars were infinite
and some stars had planets
and some didn't
there could be either
more stars than planets
or more planets than stars.
How could there possibly be
different infinities?

He dreams of her often
as a baby wrapped in that
soft pink blanket
with its silken edge,
the white and gold cot.

When he comes close
she wakes and asks him,
How many stars, Daddy?
How many stars are there?
and when he tells her
that he doesn't know
she shrinks away
and the cot is empty.

Marlo and the bowled dog

Marlo looked around quickly
after hearing a loud yelp
and saw a dog rolling over
and over and over.

It had curled itself into
a ball for self-protection
and had bounced and bounced
from the road over the footpath
and into a fence.
That was the awful bit,
the little brown and white dog
bouncing like a grubber kick.

A boy jumped off his pushbike
and ran towards it.
The dog stayed rolled in a ball
with its tail tucked in
between its legs
and whimpering
but it moved its head up
to lick the boy's hand.

Marlo went over to them
and the kid asked firmly,
Did you get his number, mister?
Marlo had to say that
he hadn't even noticed
which car had hit the dog
and no one had stopped.

The dog stood up at last.
Shaking and trembling,
it took a few steps
then flopped to the footpath
like a tent coming down
and began to lick
one of its back legs.

We'd better get him to a vet,
said Marlo.
The kid said his mother wasn't home yet
but Marlo persuaded him
to let him drive them to the vet.

The vet ran her hands
all over the dog,
found no broken bones
and the little dog
didn't wince
when she pushed her fingers
into his abdomen
and around his rib cage.

So with a comforting nod she said,
It should be all right.
Just heavy bruising.

Then Marlo drove
the kid and his dog
back to their home,
a run-down house
rented by a single mother.
He told her not to worry,
he'd fixed up the vet.

It's OK, he assured her,
it wasn't much.
I don't mind.
Don't worry about it.

Sherry

Sherry had treated Limpet
since she was a kitten.
Limpet would lock on
to Sherry's arm
like a benign alien;
a grey and white growth
radiant with approval
infusing love vibes.

But today Sherry had helped
Limpet to the sleep
from which no cat wakes
and Sherry cried
after Limpet's sad owner
took her home to be part
of his garden forever.

No man had ever wanted Sherry;
used yes, wanted no;
men at parties ignored her
or would talk to her
but never sought more than talk.
It seemed she'd stopped
being interested in men long ago
and made do with the more honest
love of the higher animals.

Among Limpet's last day
were the predictable de-sexings
and a few more sad things
and an overweight cat
but some happy reunions
and a man brought in a kid
with a dog hit by a car.
Not me of course, said Marlo.
Defensive old turd, thought Sherry.
No, said the kid,
it wasn't him.

Marlo explained what had happened
and said he'd pay for the treatment –
X-rays antibiotics et cetera –
with a kind of insincere
suppressed attitude of
oh-no-don't-thank-me.

Sherry straight away
sensed X-rays were not needed
and didn't need one smug,
I've-got-it-under-control
middle-aged-fart male-person
to tell her how to treat a dog.

She could look into the dog's eyes
and sense things about him.
She could feel him and know
the joints and the paws
and their movements.
A gentle trailing along the spine,
her fingers softly pressing
around the ribcage
and the abdomen
and the discharge areas
and the dog's reaction
said no broken bones,
no internal damage.
She teased out urine and faeces.

It should be all right;
just heavy bruising,
a bit of shock as well.
He'll be all right.
He's been a lucky little dog,
she assured the kid.

Still the questioning
from the oh-so-caring man,
Are you sure?
She nodded and smiled,
restrained herself.

Marlo took care of what
he called *the formalities.*

After they'd gone
Sherry told the vet nurse,
No one, and I mean no one,
does largesse
with quite the same smugness
as a middle-class
middle-aged man
with a bit in the bank.

Marlo and the dero

Marlo heard a solid
chunky percussion
of bone on concrete.
An old homeless man
drinking against the wall
had passed out,
fallen right over
and his head
played drum
on the footpath.

Marlo bent down
to straighten him up.
The old bloke's head was heavy
like a cat's head after death.

Another man passing by
stopped to help,
young, tall, strong;
the kind that likes
to be in charge.
Here, I'll fix it.
He straightened the dero
against the wall.
*How are you going, mate
all right?*

Marlo nearly answered
as if the question
had been asked to him
but stopped himself
then almost said,
Excuse me,
I'm saving the old bloke.
Piss off green brain.
But he held off
for the crusader was
young, strong and decisive.
Not much else we can do.
He'll sleep it off.
You don't know him do you?

Marlo shook his head.

Oh well, there but – as they say.

Only after the young alpha
had walked definitively on
did Marlo notice
the retchy stink about the dero,
that his pants were pissy wet
and that he'd passed out
with his fingers closed tightly
around the open top
of his sherry bottle.

There was still about
a quarter of it left –
enough for a heart starter.
Marlo tucked the bottle
tightly beside the dero's elbow
and bunched his old khaki coat
around it before stroking him
on the shoulder,
slipping a twenty
into one of his pockets
and walking away.

You make your own luck

Late thirties man late twenties
woman at a restaurant table
leaning forward to each other.

Decisiveness that's the thing.
You make the decision. Don't
let the decision make you.

She likes to hear this man talk,
likes it more that he has the runs
on the board to back it up.

Do you ever notice, she asks,
how even at the lowest level
some people will stand back.

Yeah, I have. Why do they do that?
She's as strong as gravity.
He moves his hand across to hers.

The waiter interrupts with soup,
fusses about with the wine.
She lifts her hand: *Leave it!*

He mimics her hand motion.
I like a girl who won't take any
number two from waiters.

She takes in the smooth soup
in a delicate feminine way.
He's just coming over to perve.

He slows himself to match her,
about to suggest they clink spoons,
thinks again – far too corny.

Out of the blue she starts to tell him,
Some old lady fell down near the library,
missed her footing on the stone stairs.

People just watched – as I was saying
earlier – but I went over to help her up.
She was so grateful – all over me.

He smiles knowingly: *Same thing*
on my way here – an old wino,
complete with army overcoat,

sort of collapsed. His head hit the concrete.
Awful sound. Some Middle-Age-Fart
just kept looking at him.

I stepped in and straightened
him up, checked his head and neck.
He was all right. I think the M-A-F

would have kept looking for hours.
She cut in, *He probably still is mate.*
The poodles are lucky we're around.

They raise their glasses, their hopes,
their eyes are getting drunk.
Their hands squeeze monkey fashion.

The waiter brings the lamb,
bids them, *Enjoy.* She thanks him,
then mouths *Enjoy* to her power man.

They laugh. She stretches her leg
forward and touches his. *Sorry,* she lies.
He searches out hers under the table.

Their hands resume monkey grip.
They try to eat only with the other one.
Something circular has started

as basic as the orbiting motions
of atoms and planets legs bodies
fingers eyes legs bodies fingers

eyes Venus asteroids Pluto.
The waiter, the bloody waiter.
Yes. We're right. Leave us.

Marlo visits old Ec

Visiting an older dying
friend in a hospice
Marlo thinks of all the knowledge
his friend will no longer need,
how all those things
he'd learned over the years
won't matter any more;

the hard-acquired facts,
algebra, Latin, the names of bones,
the great wall of China,
the moons circling Jupiter:
all of little subsequent use,

not to mention sixty-plus years
of good and bad song lyrics.
How much of our brain,
he wonders, is filled with
those unforgettable songs,
Procul Harem, Little Heroes.

So much to pick up in a life:
red bikes go faster,
the unions have too much power,
big business has too much power,
a woman'll never leave her baby,
drive nails in skew for a better grip,
check the brake fluid level.

Lost in these thoughts
of all this practical learning
Marlo has let the older man's
words trickle on until
he suddenly realises
he hasn't been listening:
Sorry mate what was that?

Old Ec repeats
what he'd been saying.
He is one of those who
on the final bed will talk a lot
to put his visitors at ease.

A young nurse comes in
and checks his pills.

They've no idea, have they?
Old Ec suggests.
They'll have no idea until they get here.

The visit draws on until
the dying man grows tired
and talks himself out.

Marlo finds it hard to ask.

His old friend tells him anyway.

Might last a month or two,
might go tomorrow.
However long or short it is
they can't throw me out;
quite serious Catholics here
angel wings and holy water
immensely selfless and

he holds the word back
for a second or two…
unjudging.

The visit ends with Old Ec
squeezing Marlo's hands
with something like a benediction.

When he leaves the hospital
and walks heavily back
to his own world
Marlo remembers
the warmth and life
in the hands of his old friend
and thinks to himself
how that tight and long-held squeeze
may well be another one
of those important things
we all have to learn.

Old Ec on politics

He turned to his grandson:
Wally I want you to get me
a Labor Party membership form.

I've seen the light – gonna join
the revolution – c'arn the workers!
His daughter tried to calm him: *Dad!*

He went on, *If someone's gotta*
bloody die – better one of those
useless clowns than one of us!

The death bed. The final bed.
A stage where the incumbent
plays to his captive audience

and a place of worship where
daughters and grandsons
bow their heads in reverence

and follow all his wildest whims.
It is a boat too. The oldest boat.
One we'll all be boarding.

That doctor who just walked past
could push it from the bank except
perhaps for too much conscience.

I'm a lucky bastard, you know,
to have you two and the brood.
Guess who called in the other day?

Gough Whitlam, said his daughter.
*Jesus, girlie, wherever did you get
your capacity for bullshit from?*

From you, Dad. The old man laughed.
*No! It was that Italian accountant
lived next door years back, Marlo.*

*He told me his middle daughter
Emily, that's it, Emily, went away
up to Brisbane to do nursing*

*and they never hear from her.
She's never once come down to visit.
No phone calls. No letters. Nothing.*

Four years now, he said. *Imagine
what that would do to you.
So I mean it – I'm a lucky bastard.*

*Don't worry about the Labor Party
Wally, it was just a bad joke, mate.*
Wally pushed in to his mum's side.

*We'll get back. The people aren't fools.
They'll realise they're being conned
by this big spending rabble.*

*Anyway you lot better get on.
I'm tired from all this talking
and entertaining you.*

His daughter smiled. *You always
loved an audience, Dad. Shake hands
with grandpa before we go, Wally.*

Wally moves closer to the bed.
The handshake is firm on both sides
and Old Ec has trouble letting go.

*That's a good firm hand you've got
there, boy. It's half the battle in life,
Wally, a firm handshake.*

*It lets the other bloke know
you feel good about yourself
and that, boy, that's the main thing.*

Emily's day

began with waking
in a more ordinary way
now that she was out of
the nurses' quarters
and living in a flat with friends.

She kept saying they could
squeeze another one in
and lower the rent for each of them:
more money for the future.

The future costs money
and nurses didn't get enough
for a future.
There were as many women
doctors as men now
so marrying a doctor
was a reduced option.

She sometimes thought
of her sisters, that they'd
leave as soon as they could.

She was having second thoughts
about the motorcycle now,
the cost and the danger:
more the cost than the danger.

She'd always get some work
nursing overseas but had to get there
and had to have enough to get back.
She was definitely not
going to be like her friend,
Allison, and ring her parents
for airfare back.

No way! This trip was going
to be fully funded:
more than any election promise.
The ordinariness of the day
was both reassuring and boring.
The breakfast. The shower.
The bus. The ward. The head sister.
The roster. The patients,
their gratitude, their warmth,
their quiet flirting.

There was one only last week
a teenage girl who reminded her
of her younger sister Kylie;
same face shape and same laugh,
same colour hair;
even had the same name.

Tending to her
brought up the old question again
and she still can't decide
whether or not to let her mother
know when she goes overseas.

Marlo dances with Kylie

At the wedding of one of the friends
of their eldest daughter, Antonia,
Marlo and his wife
had given their best possible
impression of a waltz
to a slow song from the sixties
(Humperdinck) and then sat down
quickly when the music had sped up
and several songs went by
which they vaguely recognised
as having been hummed, sung
and downloaded by all their daughters.

It was especially at celebrations
like this that gathered in
any family's private diaspora,
the interstate cousins,
the doctor from Perth and so on
that he missed their middle daughter, Emily.
He would automatically include her
in a painful phrase like
our three daughters…

It was as if Kylie, the youngest,
could sense beyond her years
how much he was hurt
when Emily left home
that she suggested they dance.
He didn't really want to
given that she was changing
and they were touching less
and she stayed in her room more.
He was scared she'd go as well.

Then the band announced
they'd play one for the real oldies:
'I'll take you home again Kathleen'.
Kylie pulled him to his feet and
dragged him to the dance floor.
Such strength, he thought,
in her back and her –
he could hardly allow himself
to say it – her hips and her…

*It's all right, Dad – see – Rebecca's
dancing with her father.*
So he held her awkwardly
fighting the urge to cling to her
and closed his eyes and pretended
it was Emily –
the fifth who walks beside us –
as he described her in his mind.

They moved and shuffled slowly.
Kylie would look up and smile at him
and then around the room at everyone,
aglow with pride,
and mouthing to some of her friends:
my father Fred Astaire.

The song ended.
They let their arms fall
and walked back to the table together.
Marlo was glad to be sitting
as he felt the blackness moving in,
felt Kylie kiss him on the cheek
then watched her rush off
to talk with her friends.
He squeezed the tears back in,
held them back,
stopped them somehow.

www.ingramcontent.com/pod-product-compliance
Lightning Source LLC
Chambersburg PA
CBHW070954080526
44587CB00015B/2308